Counting My Blessings

111 Reasons Why I Am Thankful

Presented
To

_____

From

_____

On This Day

_____

About this Book

Most of us have heard at some point, the words "Count Your Blessings". Whether they came from a caring parent, friend or pastor, you may have allowed it to just go into one ear and out of the other. Now, more than ever, is the time to take those three words seriously. With so much crime, sickness, poverty and heartache in the world, we should all take a stand to focus on the positive things in our lives and in the world. We are constantly being fed bad news via the mass media, well intentioned family and friends and even in our email inbox 24 hours a day, 7 days a week. Not only that but also having to deal with our daily personal disappointments, frustrations, crises and losses.

Thousands of years ago, Titus Livius said "Men are slower to recognize blessings, than misfortunes". I find that to be true still today, individually and as a society. It is time to reverse that kind of thinking. Even with all the negativity and tragedies in the world there are so many things to be thankful for. If you are able to read this you are blessed. So many people cannot see to read or they may not have the mental capability to do so. Not that we should only feel blessed in the event of other's adversities. But it puts things into perspective so that we will not take certain things for granted, but to see them as the miracles they are. We are all walking, living, breathing blessings - to ourselves and to others.

If you're still not convinced, a 2003 article in the *Journal of Personality and Social Psychology* titled *Counting Blessings Versus Burdens: An Experimental Investigation of Gratitude and Subjective Well-Being In Daily Life* examines the effect of a grateful outlook on psychological and physical well being based upon a well documented study. The findings were astounding. Results suggested that a conscious focus on blessings may have emotional and interpersonal benefits.

This book, your book, *Counting My Blessings*, will help you to get to that point by allowing you to simply list and elaborate on the things in your life that you consider to be a blessing. While it is understood that God has blessed each of us in so many ways that we can't possibly count them all, we can at least start to focus on those blessings that we can identify on a daily basis. The pages in this book were intentionally left blank without lines so that you could express your blessings in the way you would like. If you want to write them, you can. If you are artistic and want to draw your blessings, you can. Or you can cut and paste pictures of your blessings or any combination of all of those. This is your book to create the way you want to. But the most important thing is to acknowledge your blessings and give birth to new ones. Don't forget to include things that may be frustrating or disappointing to you at this time. They could be blessings in disguise.

After taking this spiritual journey you will be amazed at how many seemingly simple things/blessings we take for granted each day and at the same time you will be overjoyed to know how blessed you truly are. The real miracle is that you will start looking at things differently and start feeling a peace you may have never felt before. Also, you will have the opportunity to come up with ways to bless others in the "Bless It On" section at the end. This could change your life as well as the lives of others.

On the internet, many things have been counted – from webpage pixels, hits on YouTube to pounds. Once you have counted all or some of your 111 blessings, please join us on this miraculous journey by visiting www.blessingsamillion.com to count and share your blessings with the rest of the world.

This is your book. Yes, you are the author. Use a pen, such as a Sharpie fine line permanent marker, to write your name in the space provided on the front. Over the next several pages you will embark upon a joyous journey that will help you to create your very own "Blest Seller".

Happy Blessings,
I. M. Blest

My Blessings

Reflect upon your present blessings, of which every man has plenty; not on your past misfortunes, of which all men have some.

—Charles Dickens

Blessing
1

Blessing
2

Blessing
3

Blessing
4

Blessing
5

Blessing
6

Blessing
7

Blessing
8

Blessing
9

Blessing
10

Blessing
11

Blessing
12

Blessing
13

Blessing
14

Blessing
15

Blessing
16

Blessing
17

Blessing
18

Blessing
19

Blessing
20

Blessing
21

Blessing
22

Blessing
23

Blessing
24

Blessing
25

Blessing
26

Blessing
27

Blessing
28

Blessing
29

Blessing
30

Blessing
31

Blessing
32

Blessing
33

Blessing
34

Blessing
35

Blessing
36

Blessing
37

Blessing
38

Blessing
39

Blessing
40

Blessing
41

Blessing
42

Blessing
43

Blessing
44

Blessing
45

Blessing
46

Blessing
47

Blessing
48

Blessing
49

Blessing
50

Blessing
51

Blessing
52

Blessing
53

Blessing
54

Blessing
55

Blessing
56

Blessing
57

Blessing
58

Blessing
59

Blessing
60

Blessing
61

Blessing
62

Blessing
63

Blessing
64

Blessing
65

Blessing
66

Blessing
67

Blessing
68

Blessing
69

Blessing
70

Blessing
71

Blessing
72

Blessing
73

Blessing
74

Blessing
75

Blessing
76

Blessing
77

Blessing
78

Blessing
79

Blessing
80

Blessing
81

Blessing
82

Blessing
83

Blessing
84

Blessing
85

Blessing
86

Blessing
87

Blessing
88

Blessing
89

Blessing

Blessing
91

Blessing
92

Blessing
93

Blessing
94

Blessing
95

Blessing

Blessing
97

Blessing
98

Blessing
99

Blessing
100

Blessing 101

Blessing
102

Blessing
103

Blessing
104

Blessing
105

Blessing
106

Blessing
107

Blessing
108

Blessing
109

Blessing
110

Blessing
111

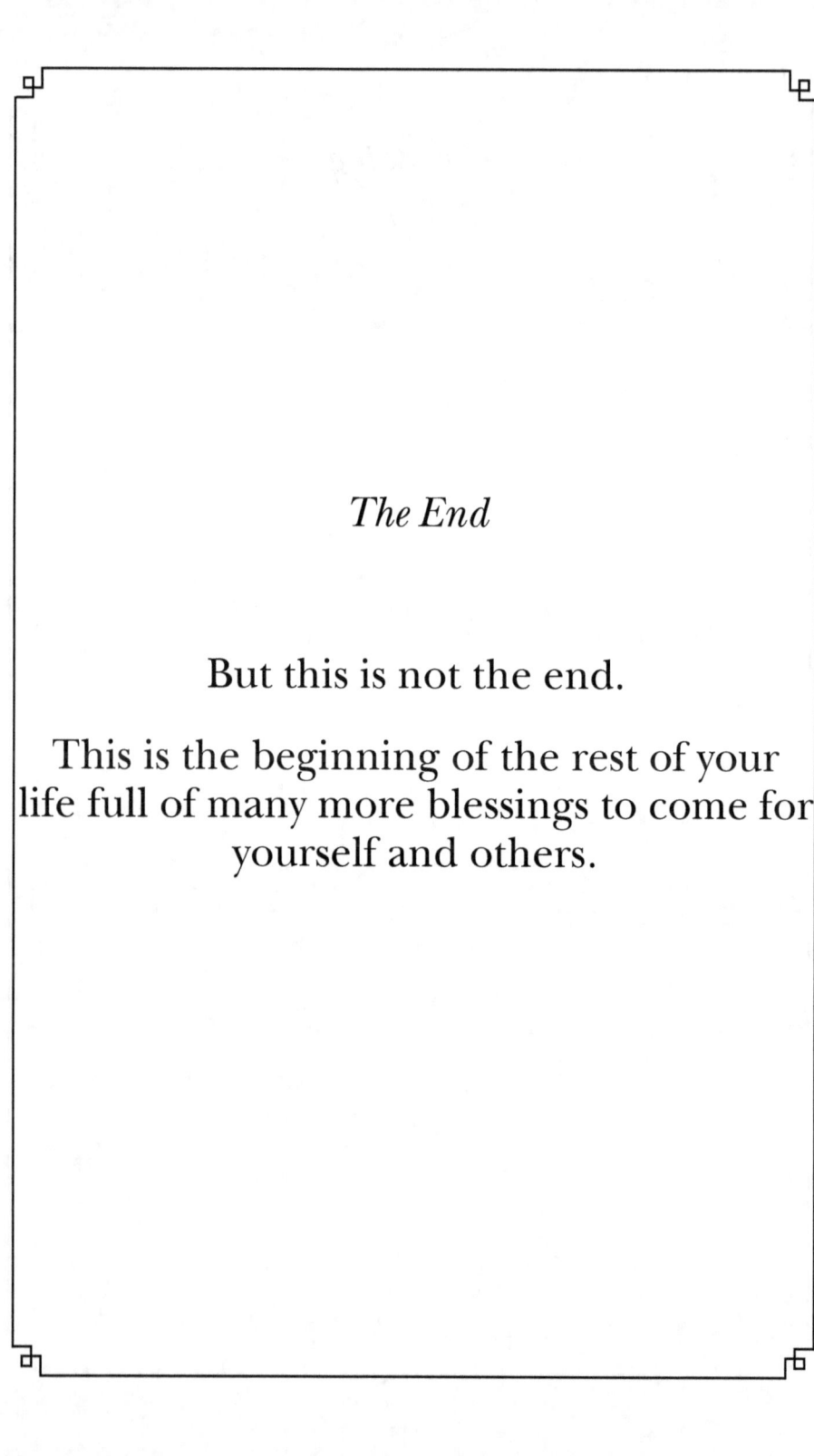

The End

But this is not the end.

This is the beginning of the rest of your life full of many more blessings to come for yourself and others.

Bless It On

Bless It On

Use the following pages to write the names of people or groups of people you can bless in some way. You can also explain how you will bless them. It can be a simple gesture such as just giving someone a compliment to make them smile or you could bless someone financially in need as much as your budget or creativity will allow.

Happy Blessings!

Bless It On
1

Who:

How:

Bless It On
2

Who:

How:

Bless It On
3

Who:

How:

Bless It On
4

Who:

How:

Bless It On
5

Who:

How:

Bless It On
6

Who:

How:

Bless It On
7

Who:

How:

Bless It On
8

Who:

How:

Bless It On
9

Who:

How:

Bless It On
10

Who:

How: